Reptile Keeper's Guides

THE COLL
Landbeach Roa
Tel: (0

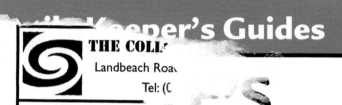

E'S

AND

WHITE-LIPPED TREEFROGS

R. D. Bartlett
Patricia Bartlett

BARRON'S

Acknowledgments

Several people have helped us in numerous ways with this book. We extend our thanks to Rob MacInnes, Mike Stuhlman, Chuck Hurt, and B. J. Kulick of Glades Herp; to Bill Love of Blue Chameleon Ventures; to Mike and Lisa Manfredi, and to Jim Harding for generously sharing information and photographic opportunities with us. Our gratitude as well goes to Dave Schleser and Dave Roberts, and to our editor, Pat Hunter, for their thoughtful help on this manuscript.

All inquiries should be addressed to:
Barron's Educational Series, Inc.
250 Wireless Boulevard
Hauppauge, New York 11788
http://www.barronseduc.com

International Standard Book No. 0-7641-1700-9

Library of Congress Catalog Card No. 2001035314

Library of Congress Cataloging-in-Publication Data
Bartlett, Richard D., 1938–
    White's and white-lipped treefrogs : facts & advice on care
and breeding / R. D. Bartlett.
        p.   cm.—(Reptile keeper's guides)
    ISBN 0-7641-1700-9
    1. White's treefrogs as pets.   2. White-lipped treefrogs
as pets.   I. Title.
SF459.F83   B39 2001
639.3'7878—dc21   2001035314

Printed in Hong Kong
9 8 7 6 5 4 3 2 1

Contents

Preface

It was more than 40 years ago when I (Dick) first became acquainted with and enchanted by the White's treefrog, *Litoria caerulea*, a species of Australia and New Guinea. At that time, its larger relative, the white-lipped treefrog, *L. infrafrenata*, primarily of New Guinean origin, had not yet become available. In fact, it was only in the mid-1980s that the latter species was seen with any regularity in the United States. Over the years, the availability of both species has varied dramatically. At some times they have been common; at other times they have been difficult to acquire, but currently (at the turn of the 21st century) both are readily available.

Because hobbyists are now breeding them, White's treefrogs probably will not become truly uncommon in

A White's treefrog rests.

the pet trade again, nor should they again be expensive. However, because we have not yet learned the secrets needed to regularly breed in captivity the somewhat harder to keep white-lipped treefrogs, the pet industry is still largely dependent on wild-collected specimens. Such dependency, coupled with changing wildlife laws, almost guarantees unstable availability and costs.

White's and white-lipped treefrogs are now among the most popular of hylid frogs with hobbyists. They are the only two kinds (out of almost 100 species) in the genus *Litoria* to have gained this popularity. Currently, wildlife exportation restrictions in Australia limit the availability of other desirable forms.

Although both the White's and the white-lipped treefrogs are among the most easily handled of frogs, we still consider them "just to look at" terrarium animals. If it becomes necessary to handle either, wash your hands thoroughly both before and after. Washing your hands before you handle these frogs protects the frogs; washing your hands afterward protects you. (See page 15 for comments on frog skin toxicity.)

Because of the ease with which it may be maintained and its ready availability, White's treefrog is often the species that hobbyists keep first, expanding their horizons to the related white-lipped treefrog only after a period of success with the former. We hope that the information in this book will provide hobbyists with a better understanding of both species.

Dick and Patti Bartlett

Introduction

How, or why, a reptile or amphibian becomes an icon in the pet industry has never failed to perplex us. Some species, relatively obscure at the time, catch the interest of a few commercial breeders, who then go to great lengths to popularize the creature. At the same time, a more readily available and seemingly equally interesting and pretty species will be all but ignored by breeders and hobbyists alike. The former scenario was the case with the White's (or dumpy) treefrog, and seems now to be happening with the white-lipped treefrog.

White's (*Litoria caerulea*) and white-lipped treefrogs (*Litoria infrafrenata*; some researchers place both frogs in the genus *Pelodryas*) are large Australian and Indonesian treefrogs or hylids. Of the two, White's has been around longer and is familiar to most reptile and amphibian hobbyists. White's first became available in the

A portrait of a White's treefrog.

United States in the early 1950s. At that time, they were imported directly from Australia, at a cost of only a few dollars each, and even then were considered quite inexpensive.

What I saw when I first viewed those imported White's treefrogs were several hefty little frogs (they were all about 2 inches [5 cm] in length), tidily clad in a smooth, jade-green skin. They sat quietly, eyes abug, probably wondering in their limited froggy way what exactly was going on. All survived for years in our terrariums, but none was bred. Nobody knew anything about breeding snakes, much less frogs, at that time.

Shortly after the arrival of those frogs, Australia closed its borders to the exportation of wildlife and White's treefrogs suddenly became a thing of the past. During those years of reduced availability (almost 20 years passed before the frog was again seen in the pet trade), the very few White's treefrogs that became available were commanding prices of more than $100 each.

A White's treefrog rests on the leaf of an orchid.

However, during those years of slim availability, a few herpetoculturists began looking critically at White's treefrogs. A few had been bred in Germany and their offspring sometimes were imported into the United States. Here, herpetoculturists began experimenting with a few readily available American treefrog species to find the parameters that best suited the reproductive cycling of treefrogs. Then those lessons were applied to White's treefrogs. Despite the fact that White's treefrog came from half a world and a full hemisphere away, the newly learned practices stood herpetoculturists in good stead. White's treefrogs did not prove difficult to breed in considerable quantities.

First bred in naturalistic greenhouse setups, it was only a matter of time before we learned to use hydration chambers and smaller terrariums to induce breeding in White's treefrogs. As a result, production increased remarkably. Today (mid-2001), White's treefrogs are readily available and the prices again have dropped into a very affordable $15 to $35 range.

This regulation and market-driven fluctuation in prices demonstrates the importance of herpetoculture. Before White's treefrogs were protected by Australia, the frogs were inexpensive. When conservation measures were invoked and enforced, the price spiraled upward. Commercially practical captive-breeding programs then were developed, which assured that additional frogs from the wild were not necessary. These programs actually provided more White's treefrogs for the pet market than were ever before available. These captive-hatched young were already

The namesake white lip of the white-lipped treefrog is a distinctive field mark.

adapted to captivity and to captive diets, consisting of easily procured insects.

The white-lipped has proven somewhat more difficult to acclimate to captivity than the White's treefrog. Although a popular treefrog, its presence in our hobby is largely dependent upon wild-collected specimens. The longevity of the white-lipped treefrog in captivity only rarely has exceeded four years. In contrast, the White's treefrogs have a typical captive longevity in excess of 10 years, and some have lived more than 20 years. Obviously, our techniques with the white-lipped treefrogs need a little more work.

Certainly, part of the problem

with the white-lips is that they are taken from the wild. Field-collected animals often are stressed by capture. The delicate balance between internal parasites and the animal's health is skewed, and what had been a manageable parasite load develops into an untenable amount. We suggest that a veterinary assessment of your new white-lipped treefrogs' condition, and follow-up treatments (when necessary), be routinely given.

Both the White's and the white-lipped treefrogs frequently exceed 2.5 inches (6 cm) in length, and some individuals (usually females) may measure 4 to 5 inches (10 to 13 cm) long, perhaps reason enough for their popularity with hobbyists.

What Are White's and White-Lipped Treefrogs?

Both White's and white-lipped treefrogs are large and heavy-bodied members of the family Hylidae (the true treefrogs). The females of both are the larger sex. Some female White's treefrogs attain 4 inches (10 cm) in svl (snout-vent length), and an occasional female white-lipped treefrog may attain a 5-inch (13-cm) size. Males are smaller, at about a 2.5- to 3-inch (6- to 8-cm) body length. Both species have toepads and climb very well.

White's Treefrog

The large size, green coloration, and propensity toward corpulence have given rise to several additional vernac-ular names for the White's treefrog. Among these are Australian green, giant green, and dumpy treefrog. The females of this species tend to develop heavy supratympanal folds—folds in the skin above the eyes, rather like great hairless eyebrows—that are quite distinctive. In some particularly old and obese specimens, these ridges may become so enlarged and pendulous that they actually droop over at least part of the eye, partially obscuring vision. Both sexes have a short, rounded nose.

White's treefrogs are very hardy and long-lived. Many captives have established records of 15 to 20 years, and it is probable that more than 25 years could be attained.

The huge toepads of the White's treefrog ensure a strong grasp.

This White's treefrog is bluer in color than most.

way that wax protects your furniture. The restricted loss of body moisture allows the White's treefrog to colonize drier areas than are possible for many other treefrogs. In addition to being better able to deal with drier conditions than other frogs, White's treefrogs from the southern part of the range have proven to be cold tolerant. As would be expected, those from the more tropical areas of northern Australia and Indonesia are more cold-sensitive and must be kept warm throughout the year.

When in their green color phase, White's treefrogs often tend toward a jade green coloration. However, in life these frogs also may vary from olive to olive-brown, or occasionally to blue.

Preserved White's treefrogs are also blue. Since scientific descriptions most often are based on preserved specimens, this may explain how the specific scientific name of "caerulea" (Latin for "blue") was derived. It has been shown that the blue coloration of living White's treefrogs may be caused by a diet deficient somewhat in beta-carotene.

Like other amphibians and reptiles in herpetoculture, new colors and patterns are considered very desirable/marketable. Some specimens of White's treefrogs bear white spots on their back. Herpetoculturists are now line-breeding specimens in an attempt to increase the amount of white.

The glandular dorsal skin of White's treefrogs is smooth and desiccation-resistant. The dessication resistance is partially due to lipids secreted by the skin that essentially seal in the moisture, in much the same

White-Lipped Treefrog

Even larger than the White's treefrog, the white-lipped treefrog, a species with rougher skin, is continuing to gain in hobbyist popularity. The white-lipped treefrog is a more tropical species and is dependent on a constant supply of moisture to sustain life. The white-lipped treefrog has not yet been bred with any consistency. In fact, in most cases the white-lipped treefrog has proven somewhat difficult to maintain over an extended period. Most likely, this is because those specimens available in the pet trade are collected from the wild, and most seem to harbor unhealthy concentrations of endoparasites.

Like White's treefrog, the white-lipped treefrog can change its coloration. Although it is often a bright green (especially at night when it is active), the same frog may assume an olive-green, olive-brown, or deep brown coloration. The darker colors are most often seen by day when the white-lipped treefrog is normally inactive. The color of an individual

Normally quiet during the day, white-lipped treefrogs become alert and active after nightfall.

specimen is usually directly related to surrounding environmental conditions and to stress. Those maintained in warm, uncrowded terraria seem to retain their green coloration, while a specimen kept in cool, crowded, or otherwise suboptimal surroundings becomes darker in color.

The white lower lip is well in evidence on this appropriately named frog. The belly is white to off-white and, like the green sides, is strongly granular. Supratympanal folds (folds of skin over the external eardrum) are present, but are not overly developed. They do not involve the upper eyelid. A light stripe is present on the inner edge of each tibia. This becomes suffused with peach color on breeding males.

Both species have very large toe-pads and climb well.

The ranges of the White's treefrog and the white-lipped treefrog differ. White's treefrog may be encountered in suitable habitats throughout the

northern half of Australia and in southern New Guinea. Subtle morphological differences between the New Guinean and Australian populations indicate that these populations have long been discrete.

The range of the more tropical white-lipped treefrog is limited in Australia to coastal regions of Queensland's Cape York Peninsula, but it also occurs widely on New Guinea, on islands in the Torres Strait, and on other nearby islands and island clusters.

It seems that the White's treefrog has benefited greatly by following human settlement into what would have been otherwise unsuitable habitats. This large treefrog climbs agilely and may thus find the moisture it needs to survive, and perhaps even to breed, in areas not available to terrestrial frogs. In natural habitats, White's treefrogs may be found near any area that retains water, in habitats as diverse as rocky escarpments and sclerophyll forests.

Although the white-lipped treefrog is more restricted to forested areas within its range, it may also be found in natural and human altered habitats.

Despite being quiet most of the time, both White's and white-lipped treefrogs occasionally become ambulatory. They both walk in a hand-over-hand manner along their arboreal highways, but if startled they make some unexpectedly rapid and lengthy leaps.

The territorial (and breeding) calls of White's treefrog consist of a single, harsh, often repeated croak. The calls of the white-lipped treefrog are two-syllabled.

Besides the White's and the white-lipped treefrogs, three other species of the genus *Litoria* also are occasionally available. Two of these, *L. raniformis* and *L. aurea* (known respectively as the blue-thighed bell frog and the green and golden bell frog), are very similar in appearance and look more like true, non-arboreal frogs than treefrogs. The third, *L. chloris*, is a beautiful, small treefrog of typical appearance that is green to cream in color and has coppery irises bearing a red outer ring. It is called the Australian red-eyed treefrog.

Both of the bell frogs are primarily a warm, golden brown on their back and sides, but both have irregular patches of green on their face, between the eyes, and above the dorso-lateral ridges. The green borne by the blue-thighed bell frog tends to be more extensive and darker than that of the green and golden bell frog. The former also tends to have more rugose, or textured, upper sides (above the dorsolateral ridges), and at a

Although looking more like a typical frog than a treefrog, the green and golden bell frog, *L. aurea*, is nonetheless a relative of the White's and white-lipped treefrog.

The blue-thighed bell frog, *L. raniformis*, is usually very richly colored.

length of 3 inches (8 cm), it is the larger of the two.
The call of neither is particularly reminiscent of the bell
to which the common names allude.

Both of these species are extensively aquatic, and
often seek shelter beneath water-edge debris or vegetation overhanging the water. The green and golden bell
frog occurs in eastern New South Wales and extreme
northeastern Victoria. The blue-thighed bell frog ranges
from southern interior New South Wales and southeastern South Australia southward through Victoria and
Tasmania. These are pretty and hardy frogs, which are
occasionally bred in captivity, especially by European
hobbyists.

The skin color of the Australian red-eyed treefrog, *L. chloris*, varies from cream to rich green.

The Australian red-eyed treefrog is very arboreal. Both the fingers and the toes are extensively webbed. It attains a length of about 2 inches (5 cm). This pretty frog is bred by both American and European hobbyists. It occurs in woodlands and fields, in coastal Queensland and New South Wales, Australia.

Although all three of these frogs are more difficult to acquire than either the White's or the white-lipped treefrogs, they are occasionally available in the pet trade. All are hardy, feed well on a variety of insects, and can be expected to live for more than five years in captivity.

White's and White-Lipped Treefrogs as Pets

Unlike reptiles, amphibians have been slow to gain popularity in the pet field. There are probably less than a dozen species that could be considered long-term favorites, and then another couple of dozen that are seen with a reasonable degree of regularity. This is probably because as a group, amphibians do require more care than reptiles, and they sicken more quickly when their needs are not met.

White's treefrogs will thrive for years on a regimen of minimal amphibian care. This does not mean that they can be ignored, neglected, or allowed to dwell in a dirty container—just that their care is neither specialized nor difficult, and the frog usually can be left for a day or two without care if you are vacationing. In fact, when it comes to husbandry, White's treefrogs are among the least demanding of all amphibians. They are possessed of a quiet demeanor, are almost always ready to eat, and the somewhat comical appearance of old adults (especially old adult females) endears them to many folks who otherwise dislike herptiles.

All portions of the caging—land, water, glass, plantings, and perches in which these frogs are kept—must be free of potential pathogens. Either wash and rinse all components with a copious quantity of clean, pure water (no cleansers), or if you do use a

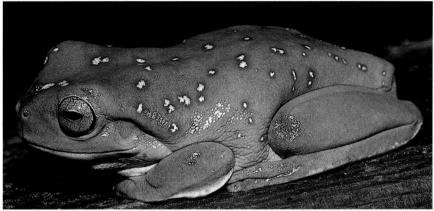

White's treefrog can be bright green at one moment, olive a few minutes later.

cleanser, opt for a very dilute solution of Clorox and water (one part Clorox to 20 parts water), then when finished, rinse, rinse, and rinse again—with clean, pure water. Never use any phenol-based cleanser in your treefrog's home.

Cage size varies with the size of its inhabitants. A few small metamorphs (newly metamorphosed froglets) can be kept in a 5- or 10-gallon (19- to 38-L) tank, but adults require a larger terrarium. A 10-gallon (38-L) terrarium is usually sufficient for one or two average size (2- to 4-inch [5- to 10-cm] length) specimens. A larger group (up to a half dozen specimens) should be housed in a 30- to 50-gallon (113- to 189-L) terrarium. In suitable weather, White's treefrogs thrive in outdoor cages of wood and wire construction (containing plants and a water dish), and are particularly at home in heavily planted greenhouses.

The desiccation-resistant, glandular skin of White's and white-lipped treefrogs allows them to inhabit areas of relatively sparse rainfall. Keep in mind that neither in the wild, nor in captivity, does a White's treefrog need, or even want, to be continually wet. However, a captive always must have access to a small dish of clean, dechlorinated water. (Dechlorinating liquids are available at your local pet or tropical fish store.) Provide numerous wide, horizontal, above-ground perches. These should be the same as, or slightly greater than, the body diameter of the frogs. Sections of giant bamboo are favored. The frogs not only will sit on top of lateral sections, but if you use a saw or a machete to open up the hollow stem, the frogs will back themselves comfortably into the niches. Although treefrogs move around a network of small diameter branches, they prefer to rest on larger and more secure perches. These (and other treefrogs) also may rest while securely adhering to the glass of the terrarium, on the upright braces of other styles of cages, or, if in a well-planted greenhouse, on the leaves or in the leaf axils of banana trees or other such large-leaf plants.

Daytime terrarium temperatures of 80 to 85°F (27 to 29°C) and nighttime lows of 68 to 75°F (20 to 24°C) are acceptable. Actually, White's treefrogs can survive temperatures considerably above and below these suggested parameters, but try to provide a comfortable range.

We have maintained the species outdoors in southwest Florida where daytime summer temperatures routinely rose to 94°F (34°C) and winter nighttime lows occasionally dropped to 45°F (7°C). In their cages of wood and wire construction, the White's treefrogs seemed to be fine. However, it was apparent that they were most alert at night when temperatures

White-lipped treefrogs grasp branches firmly.

ranged between 68 and 75°F (20 to 24°C) degrees.

Although we have not had any trouble acclimating and keeping the big white-lipped treefrog, we do know that other hobbyists and breeders have found this species problematic. This large treefrog requires a higher humidity and more readily available standing water than the White's treefrog. It is also less tolerant of cool temperatures and is somewhat more nervous and active than White's. Be certain that its caging provides areas of seclusion and visual barriers (such as plants) to give a feeling of security. Because it is more easily startled and active (adults can leap more than four feet [1 m] in a single bound), we urge that the white-lipped treefrog be supplied with larger quarters than the White's treefrog.

Maintain the white-lipped treefrog's terrarium temperature in the 68 to 85°F (20 to 29°C) range, and be wary of letting the temperature drop much below 65°F (18°C). We have found that if sustained over a period of hours, a temperature of less than 60°F (15°C) can be detrimental to the white-lipped treefrog.

Both the White's and the white-lipped treefrogs are capable of exuding considerable quantities of white, apparently noxious, skin secretions. Although this may double as anti-desiccant, it is certainly distasteful enough to discourage the attention of some predators.

Because the skin of these frogs absorb moisture, together with any impurities it might contain, hygiene is always an important issue. It is not only important that their quarters be free of impurities, but that your hands are clean when you handle these creatures.

Keep in mind that your hands will be far warmer than the temperature of the frogs' skin, and that washing your hands before you touch the frogs not only cleans your hands, but will help cool your skin temperature. Such often-used aides as hand cream, topical insecticides, insect repellents, soap, chlorine, and sunscreen are all detrimental to the health of your frogs. Some will be almost instantaneously fatal to these moist-skinned creatures. Wash and rinse your hands both before and after handling your treefrogs.

Can toxicity work the other way around? Can your treefrog's skin secretions prove harmful to you? The answer, seemingly, is no—unless you rub your eyes or other mucous membranes without first washing your hands. There is no question that the secretion from the frog will irritate mucous membranes. At one time the secretions were used medicinally to help reduce blood pressure, but it is now possible to synthesize and produce the beneficial ingredients in the laboratory without the need to sacrifice the animals.

Any branch is a perch for a White's treefrog.

Obtaining Your White's and White-Lipped Treefrogs

Although White's treefrogs often are available at neighborhood pet stores, the related white-lipped treefrogs seldom are. There are, however, numerous other sources for both species. The breeders and importers of these pretty frogs can be found on the Web and in the classified sections of hobbyist magazines. Although the babies (metamorphs) of White's treefrogs may be available only seasonally, larger specimens usually are available year-round. Since white-lipped treefrogs are not yet often captive-bred, usually only larger examples are available.

Pet Stores

Pet stores—especially those with expanded reptile departments—now often carry White's treefrogs of all sizes, and many probably would be willing to special order white-lipped treefrogs from their suppliers. We advocate purchases from neighborhood pet stores when possible because of the convenience and the ability of the customer to discuss the treefrogs in which they are interested. Such things as routine care are covered easily. There are times when, despite their efforts to provide accurate information, your pet store employee might err. In the store's defense, employees may just be repeating information given them by their supplier. Remember that your local pet store is often two—or even three or four—times removed from the initial purchase that placed the specimen in the pet trade.

Reptile and Amphibian Expos

Herp expos are now held in many larger cities across the United States and are becoming popular in Europe. It seems that there is at least one occurring at some point in the United States on any given weekend. Some are annual events; others may be biannual or quarterly. An expo is merely a gathering of dealers and breeders, all under one roof. One of the largest is the National Captive Reptile Breeders' Expo, with more than 450 exhibitors, that is held in central Florida every August. Captive-bred White's treefrogs often are available at this event. There are other expos that do not insist that all specimens exhibited be captive-bred. At these, white-lipped treefrogs also may be available.

Breeders

Breeders may vary in size from back-room hobbyists, who have produced a clutch of treefrogs more by accident than on purpose, to dedicated herpetoculturists, who produce from hundreds to thousands of babies each year. With each passing year, more and more of both of these frogs are being bred in captivity. Search for breeders in the classified or pictorial ads sections in specialty reptile and amphibian magazines. (See Helpful Information, page 45.) Breeders usually offer parasite-free, well-acclimated specimens and accurate information. Most keep accurate records on the species with which they work, and especially of the specimens in their breeding programs.

Specialty Dealers

The continuing growth in popularity of reptiles has allowed the success of many specialty dealers. These dealers often breed fair numbers of the amphibians and reptiles they offer, deal directly with other breeders (around the world), but may be direct importers as well. Specialty dealers usually try to acclimate and stabilize imported specimens before offering them for sale.

Mail-order Purchase and Shipping

Even with today's proliferation of herp expos, the expos, the larger breeders, and specialty dealers still are not readily available to many small-town hobbyists. If you live a little off the beaten path, and if your local pet store cannot accommodate your wants, mail-order may be the answer.

How does one go about ordering a treefrog by mail? How does one even learn that a particular species is available? Let's explore mail-order purchases and shipping.

There are several ways to learn of the availability of these frogs.

- **World Wide Web.** By instructing your search engine to seek "White's treefrog," "dumpy treefrog," or "white-lipped treefrog," you should find many breeders of these species. Some of the breeders post excellent photos on their web sites.
- **Classified Ads.** Dealers and hobbyists list their available livestock in the classified ads of several reptile and amphibian, and pet magazines.
- **Word of Mouth.** Ask friends and fellow enthusiasts for recommendations about the reptile dealers. Try to check their reliability by asking about them at nature centers, museums, zoos, or among hobbyist groups. Herpetology is a close-knit hobby and many dealers and hobbyists know each other.

What Next?

After learning that your potential supplier has a satisfactory reputation,

A White's treefrog in a shipping cup.

By day, White's treefrogs often seek seclusion in curling leaves.

that the supplier you have chosen is familiar with shipping and will be delighted to assist you in any way possible.

Among the things on which you and your shipper will have to agree are the method of payment and the method and date of shipping. Payment is often for the specimen(s) only. Shipping charges will be extra. The method of payment should be agreed upon, and fully understood by you, the purchaser, and the shipper at the time of ordering. Unless the shipper knows you well, it is almost certain that the specimen must be paid for in full (including boxing charges if any) prior to shipment. If you are in a hurry for the specimen, it probably will be necessary to get a money order or cashier's check to the shipper, or to supply a credit card number or wire transfer of funds to the account. Many shippers will accept personal checks, but will not ship until the check has cleared their bank (usually a week or so after deposit).

An alternate method of payment is C.O.D. However, this can be expensive and inconvenient. Most airlines accept cash only (not a check, not a credit card, not a debit card—just cash) for the C.O.D. amount, and there is a hefty surcharge (upward of $15) in addition to all other charges.

There are several options available for shipping frogs. Some are:

request a price list (often available on the Web). Decide what, if anything, you are going to purchase, and contact your supplier/shipper to finalize details.

What is involved with shipping? The shipping of amphibians is not at all the insurmountable barrier that many hobbyists initially think it to be, but it should be attempted only during good weather. ("Good" means not too hot and not too cold.) Shipping can be fairly expensive. Adult and juvenile frogs usually are placed in a deli cup with a piece of moist paper toweling, while tadpoles are shipped in deli cups in water. The cups are stabilized inside a Styrofoam shipping box, the whole thing placed in a corrugated outer box, and the trip for the frogs begins. The chances are excellent

- Express mail, door-to-door. Your shipper will require payment in advance for this service. The cost is $15 to $25.
- Airborne Express or FedEx is now used with increasing frequency. Whether these companies accept live amphibians is at the local manager's discretion. Charges are prepaid and

Nose to nose with a large White's treefrog.

vary between $15 and $40 for this convenient door-to-door service. Someone should be at your home to sign for the package when any of the door-to-door services is used.

- Air freight is available in two or three levels of service. This is the most expensive of the shipping methods and your shipment usually is held at the airport for your pickup. If your shipper suggests that air freight be used, discuss all particulars, including cost, destination airport, and schedules. If you do opt for air freight, avoid shipping on weekends or holidays when many cargo offices are closed. Pick up your shipment as quickly as possible after its arrival. This is especially important in bad weather. Learn the hours of your cargo office and whether the shipment can be picked up at the ticket counter if it arrives after the cargo office has closed.

You will have to pay for your shipment (including all C.O.D. charges and fees) before you can inspect it. Once you are given your shipment, open and inspect it before leaving the cargo facility. Unless otherwise specified, reliable shippers guarantee live delivery. However, to substantiate the existence of a problem, both shippers and airlines require that a "discrepancy" or "damage" report be made out, signed, and dated by airline personnel. In the very rare case when a problem has occurred, insist on completing and filing a claim form, and contact your shipper immediately for instructions. After the first time, you no longer will find the shipping of specimens intimidating. Understanding the system will open new doors of acquisition for you.

Caging

If you are merely keeping one or two of these treefrogs as an apartment or house pet, it is probable that you will want to keep them indoors where they are easily seen and most readily enjoyed. However, if you are keeping a number of either treefrog in hopes of breeding them, and if you have the space and caging, you may wish to keep them outside, at least during the summer months, where natural reproductive cycling—or simply a more natural lifestyle—may occur. Either indoor or outdoor maintenance is easily accomplished, and there are several designs of caging that are suitable for both applications.

All cages must be absolutely clean, escape-proof, and maintained within proper temperature parameters:

1. White's treefrogs from the southern Australian portion of the range are physiologically adapted to

A simple terrarium for a White's treefrog.

hibernate if ambient temperatures become too low. White's treefrogs from northern Australia and from Irian Jaya, and the exclusively tropical white-lipped treefrog, do not hibernate, and may be killed by low temperatures. The frustrating part is that there is no way to know where your White's treefrog originated, unless your dealer/retailer can supply the information. This is why we do not recommend you hibernate your White's treefrog unless you are certain of its area of origin, and of course, never attempt to hibernate the white-lipped treefrog.

2. White's treefrogs from southern Australia:
Night to 68°F (20°C); Day to 85°F (29°C); Suggested range: 70 to 80°F (21 to 27°C)
Extremes: Low 45°F (7°C); High 95°F (35°C)

3. White's treefrogs from northern Australia and Indonesia:
Night to 68°F (20°C); Day to 85°F (29°C). Suggested range: 70 to 80°F (21 to 27°C)
Extremes: Low, unknown but no lower than 65°F (18°C) suggested; High 95°F (35°C)

4. White's treefrogs, origin unknown:
Night to 68°F (20°C); Day to 85°F (29°C). Suggested range: 70 to 80°F (21 to 27°C)
Extremes: Low, unknown but no lower than 65°F (18°C) suggested; High 95°F (35°C)

5. White-lipped treefrogs, any origin:
Night to 68°F (20°C); Day to 85°F (29°C). Suggested range: 70 to 80°F (21 to 27°C)
Extremes: Low, unknown but no lower than 65°F (18°C) suggested; High 95°F (35°C)

These treefrogs can be kept in a variety of indoor and outdoor terarria. Indoor caging may be as simple as a 10-gallon (38-L) tank containing a small potted philodendron or pothos for decoration, a small crockery dish for water with a folded paper towel for substrate, or it can be as complex as you wish.

• A tightly lidded simple setup in a 10-gallon (38-L) terrarium

It is often obvious why the alternative name of dumpy treefrog is applied to the White's treefrog.

- A dry savanna style terrarium (White's treefrogs)
- A rain forest terrarium (white-lipped treefrog)

An outdoor cage may be of wood and wire mesh construction. Do not place a glass terrarium in the sun—within minutes it will become an oven and high temperatures will kill all inhabitants. A greenhouse cage is also suitable for these treefrogs.

White's treefrogs neither need nor prefer a great amount of moisture, or a particularly high humidity, in their terrarium. They are fully at home with a relatively dry substrate, a moderate humidity, and a small dish of clean water. Conversely, white-lipped treefrogs are adapted to areas of comparatively high rainfall and, as captives, require a continual supply of moisture and a high cage humidity. For both species, cage cleanliness is the most important aspect of their husbandry.

Both the white-lipped and White's treefrogs are nocturnal. They usually sleep soundly during the day, scrunched down, eyes tightly closed, and feet drawn in beneath them. They will awaken and become alert if the cage is misted or, if outside, a rainstorm occurs. The frogs naturally awaken and hunt at night.

Despite their heavy builds, both species of these treefrogs can jump long distances, and may do so if startled. However, as often as not, they will walk along the limbs in their enclosures in an amusing hand-over-hand, foot-over-foot manner.

Solid glass or clear, rigid, plastic covers elevate the humidity of a terrarium and prevent the escape of the frogs, but they also very effectively pre-

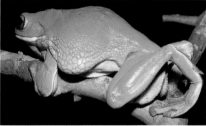

A white-lipped treefrog prepares to leap (top), ambles slowly (middle), and surveys his domain (bottom).

vent ventilation. Remember, these are not rain forest frogs. Use a screen or wire mesh top. Mist the tank once or twice daily, but ease up on the misting if you see condensation or water droplets on the sides of the tank more than a few hours after misting. If these frogs are being maintained in the arid southwestern states or in air-conditioned rooms, it will be necessary to mist the terraria more frequently than if you were in the humid southeastern states or in fog belt regions.

We suggest terraria of at least 10-gallon (38-L) capacity for one or two White's treefrogs, and at least twice that size for the same number of the more active white-lipped treefrog. If more than one or two of either species is to be kept, provide a terrarium with a capacity of from 29 to 75 gallons (109 to 284 L). Tanks of sizes greater than 10 gallons (38 L) lend themselves particularly well to naturalistic setups. Besides foliage plants, provide perches, such as sterilized driftwood or gnarled manzanita. (Do not use cedar or any limbs treated with fungicides or insecticides; both the fumes and physical contact with the wood are toxic to frogs.) Water in which your frogs can soak can be provided in an easily cleaned shallow bowl. The water receptacle should be scrubbed and fresh water provided every second or third day (more frequently if the water is dirtied). During their climbing antics, your treefrogs will smear the glass panes of their terrarium. The glass should be cleaned once or twice a week with pure water and a clean paper towel.

Since treefrogs are species that are very much utilizers of a three-dimensional habitat, we suggest that vertical-oriented terraria be provided when possible. Aquaria are now built that are as high as, or even higher than, they are long, but standard aquaria may be positioned on end to create a vertically-oriented terrarium. When this is done, use aquarium sealant to adhere a three-inch (8-cm) high strip of glass across the lower portion of the tank to prevent the gravel and soil from falling out, and to provide a suitable front.

The front cover easily can be provided by placing your terrarium on blocks or legs, an inch or two (2 to 5 cm) above the surface on which it is sitting. In a pinch, we've used 1- by 2-inch (2- by 5-cm) strips of wood. A tightly fitting framed front can then be slipped over the open side and held in place with typical top clips.

Woodland Terrarium

Woodland or forest terraria will suit the needs of most treefrogs. Both White's and the white-lipped do well in a terrarium with comparatively low humidity.

This terrarium provides only a shallow dish or two of water sunk nearly to the rim in the substrate. The multilayered land area has a base of an inch (2 cm) or so of pea-sized river rock, over which a piece of fiberglass window screening is laid. Atop this is placed from one to three inches (2 to 8 cm) of plain soil—soil containing no insecticides, fungicides, styro beads, or time-release fertilizer. Perches and plants such as philodendrons, syngoniums, spathiphyllum, and fittonias are then added, and your hylid's home is complete. If it is available, a patch of verdant woodland moss may be added.

Not all White's treefrogs bear the heavy speckling seen on this male.

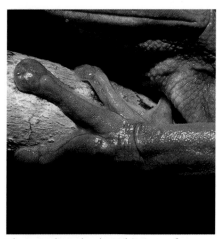

These pads make the White's treefrog surefooted in the trees.

This White's treefrog demonstrates its glass-climbing ability.

You may choose to use a substrate consisting of only a few inches of orchid bark or cypress mulch, into which the plants can be placed while still in their pots. The substrate can be washed or discarded, whichever is easier for you.

Savanna Terrarium

Savannas are defined as areas of transition between or at the edges of forest, woodland, or desert. Different soil formation and moderate rainfall provide a habitat much different from that of either surrounding desert or woodland/forest. During the dry season, these often spacious, rolling glades can appear so sparsely vegetated that they seem almost devoid of plants. However, the wet season brings about a dramatic resurgence of plant life. Almost overnight long-dormant plants—thornscrub and other formidable armed trees—regrow their leaves and green bunchgrasses and an herba-

ceous understory literally springs from the newly moistened soil.

Savannas, cloaked as they are in this seasonally diverse abundance of vegetation, are the home of many species of reptiles and amphibians not found elsewhere. It is because of the extremes of weather that savanna habitats are so difficult to reproduce. If you like a challenge, try a savanna tank; your White's treefrogs will feel right at home.

There are some easily grown succulents that can take the place of the thornscrub that is traditionally found in a savanna. Some of the various small or slow growing pachypodiums, cylindrical sanserveria, and upright euphorbias are among these. Other interesting plants would be *Ficus*, *Calibanus* (grass plant), and *Dioscorea* (tortoise foot plant). *Purslane* or portulaca is sold by nurseries for both hanging garden baskets and as bedding plants. They are drought tolerant and of succulent growth habit, but require very bright lighting. Because they are inexpensive and bear beautiful blossoms, these plants often are used as expendable terrarium plants.

Rocks, gnarled manzanita branches, corkbark hides, and perhaps a piece of cholla cactus skeleton can be incorporated into the design. A thick layer of sandy humus, into which a liberal helping of variably sized rocks has been mixed, can serve as substrate.

The plants used in the savanna terrarium can be potted or planted directly into the terrarium substrate. Certainly, it is much easier to replace potted plants than those with sprawling, unconfined root systems.

As with all other terraria, we suggest that you opt for the largest tank that you can afford and accommodate. Large terraria are easier to design and maintain than smaller ones.

Outdoor Caging

Where climatic conditions allow, outdoor caging of wood and wire can be provided for both White's and

A cage constructed of wood and wire is ideal for keeping these treefrogs outside in warm weather.

white-lipped treefrogs. The ventilation in such a cage prevents the lethal buildup of heat that would occur if glass or Plexiglas sides were used. Additionally, it permits the anurans to take limited amounts of unfiltered sun and, if the cage has a wire top, to be stimulated by falling rains. If your cage holds the xeric-adapted White's treefrog, you may need to mist only once a week. Of course, you'll need to provide a sizable receptacle of clean water, large enough for a treefrog to sit in.

Besides containing a receptacle of clean water, the cage of the white-lipped treefrog, a species adapted to damper habitats, may require misting or spraying at least once daily. When wood and wire cages are larger than tabletop size, it is prudent to incorpo-

A White's treefrog prepares to leap.

rate large casters into their design so that they may be moved about easily. In warm climates, where the treefrogs can remain outdoors for most or all of the year, we have successfully used large "step-in" caging for keeping and breeding them. The frames are of untreated 2- by 2-inch (5- by 5-cm) wood strips. The wire used is $\frac{1}{8}$-inch (.32-cm) mesh hardware cloth. The small mesh of the wire prevents the escape of all but the smallest feed crickets.

When temperatures dip, the cage can be rolled inside. If left outdoors during cool weather, the cage should be wrapped in clear 4-mil vinyl. A heat source can be added to the cage, if needed. We have used shielded light bulbs (shielded with a wire mesh screen so the frogs cannot come into direct contact with the bulb) when the temperature is "iffy." Take the cage inside if there's any doubt.

The plastic sheeting is wrapped around the cage and stapled in place on three sides. A separate piece, secured only at the top of the cage, covers the door. It can be rolled up out of the way when you need to get into the cage, or when the weather begins to warm up. In such setups, White's treefrogs will bask for hours on sunny uprights of the frame, on the horizontals of the door frame, or on the larger limbs inside. The white-lipped treefrog will remain more hidden than the White's. Remember also that the white-lipped treefrog is more sensitive to cold than the White's treefrog; temperatures that merely slow down the White's will kill the white-lipped.

The flooring of these cages can be left bare, or a low frame can be installed that will retain a clean

Hobbyists consider gold and white speckling on the back of a White's treefrog desirable.

substrate such as a sand-soil mixture, orchid bark, or cypress mulch. While we do use a soil-sand mixture on the bottoms of the cages, it is merely piled deeply and allowed to seek its own level (including being washed out) during storms. We also utilize hardy potted plants (cycads, ficus, and hanging baskets of pothos [*Epipremnum*]) within the cages. The hanging baskets serve both as decoration and visual barriers that allow the frogs to feel more secure.

Cleaning

Terrarium cleanliness will do much to ensure the long-term good health of your frogs. Regular cleaning will help prevent the spread of both diseases and endoparasites. The cleaning of terraria should be a prominent part of your husbandry regimen.

Do not use pine oil or other phenol-based disinfectants for clean-

This White's treefrog perches confidently on a light-holder above its terrarium.

ing frog cages or cage furniture. Likewise, do not use cedar mulch or furniture. Phenols, contained in both, are not tolerated well by any herps and even the lingering odors can be fatal.

Lighting and Heating

Although most amphibians do not seem to require a basking site such as the sun-basking or heliothermic reptiles do, it is probable that many derive at least some benefits from reflected UV rays. White's treefrogs, for example—a nocturnal species adapted to xeric habitats, and which, at the southern reaches of its extensive range, is also occasionally exposed to subfreezing temperatures—apparently do use a basking position, often in the direct sunlight, to thermoregulate most effectively. Other than a rapid warming, do the basking frogs derive additional benefits from the UV? We are not fully certain, but it seems probable that they do.

However, it just may be that full-spectrum lighting is actually more critical to the well-being of your terrarium plants than it is to the frogs that nestle among them. To promote photosynthesis (and growth), the use of a color-corrected "plant-grow" bulb or a full-spectrum bulb is suggested. Unless your terrarium is situated near a sunny window, even shade-dwelling forest plants, such as philodendrons and pothos, require several hours of lighting a day to thrive. Lighting is available both in incandescent and fluorescent formats.

Lighting, of course, produces a second benefit: the addition of at least a little heat. This can be very beneficial during the colder months of the year, but is less desirable during the very warm months. Incandescent bulbs produce the most heat; fluorescent bulbs, only a little, but their ballasts do produce heat. Use a timer from your local hardware store to take the "work" out of turning your lights on and off each day.

Undertank heaters, heat-tapes, and human heating pads are all readily available. Since amphibians have a delicate skin and are very subject to desiccation, a "heat rock" (basically, a heating unit within a preformed chunk of rough-surfaced cement) should never be used. If you use an undertank heater, only heat a portion—less than half—of the cage floor. The undertank heater or heating pad should be controlled by a rheostat. (See an electrician for rheostat installation if necessary.) Heat-tapes and undertank heaters are available from pet dealers; heating pads are found in drug stores. An aquarium heater in a jar of water also works. Since heated water in a small receptacle evaporates very quickly, the level of the water in which the heater is immersed must be monitored twice daily. Water poured in to replace evaporated water must be hot to the touch, to avoid breaking the glass of the aquarium heater.

An ideal daytime terrarium temperature is between 78 and 85°F (26 to 29°C). Nighttime temperatures can be several degrees cooler. It is best to provide a thermal gradient (warm to cool) within any terrarium.

Greenhouses

Although they can still be expensive, greenhouses are no longer the complete luxury items they once were. Greenhouses of many styles, constructed from several types of materials, are readily available today, and some are even relatively affordable.

Greenhouses vary from simple, self-standing, fully-constructed types available from storage shed dealers, to a myriad of do-it-yourself kits, to elaborate and decorative commercial kinds that, unless you are very "handy," are best left to contractor setup. There is, perhaps, no better caging for treefrogs than a greenhouse setup. Greenhouses usually are considered permanent structures and a building permit may be required to legally install one.

Absolute escape-proof security is essential. Escape routes are especially possible in greenhouses made of panels of corrugated fiberglass or plastic. You must ascertain that the top and bottom of every corrugation in every panel has been sealed. Some of the more inexpensive greenhouses may have the sharp tips of screws protruding into the inside. To prevent injury to jumping frogs, each protruding screw must be capped or tipped with a bead of aquarium sealant.

Additionally, in most areas of the world, heating and cooling units must be provided, and direct access to these denied, in a safe manner, to the frogs. Frogs can be cooked, desiccated, or over-chilled by improperly baffled temperature control units.

In all cases, double-glazing should be considered as an energy-saving option, especially in regions subject to extreme cold or heat. We further suggest that the base of the unit either be flush against a concrete slab, affixed to a concrete or brick wall, or be sunk a foot (30 cm) or more below the surface of the ground. This will preclude easy access by outside predators and escape by the creatures with which you are working.

It is important to provide the appropriate plantings. For White's and white-lipped treefrogs, both large species, plantings should be sturdy, as well as decorative. Some suggested species of tropical rainforest plants include philodendrons, anthuriums, selaginellas, and ficus. In time, with care, these will form wonderfully intricate tangles in which your treefrogs will feel entirely at home. Other necessities are watering, heating, and lighting systems, and cage furniture. The possibility and feasibility of providing a small pond and waterfall, often much wanted accouterments, should be discussed and implemented, if possible. Water courses can be wonderful and feasible additions to a forest-theme greenhouse that would be impossible to construct in any other setting. Your greenhouse will be a very natural and safe setting for your treefrogs because you will not be able to use an insecticide or fungicide on the plants or soil.

Feeding

Both White's and white-lipped treefrogs are large and voracious enough to eat a very wide variety of prey. Even new metamorphs are large enough to eat small crickets and wax worms. In the wild, nearly any species of non-noxious insect or other invertebrate, as well as some small vertebrates (such as other frogs), will be eaten.

We suggest that captive White's and white-lipped treefrogs be given a wide variety of healthy and healthful food items. This includes a very occasional pinky mouse. The insects fed to the frogs should always be gut loaded (fed a nutritional diet themselves) and should at least weekly be dusted with a calcium/vitamin D_3 supplement. The vitamin-mineral supplementation is especially important to the health of fast-growing baby frogs, and probably to females about to breed.

An occasional pinky mouse means just that. When a diet high in lipids (fats) is fed steadily to White's and white-lipped treefrogs, health problems can result. The two most notable are a rapid onset of obesity (no healthier for a frog than for a human) and corneal opacities that can cause blindness and are apparently irreversible. However, after a winter's cooling, the feeding of one or two pinky mice a week (in addition to a normal diet of insects) for a month will allow your treefrogs to quickly regain any lost weight. After a month, drop the frequency with which you feed pink mice down to no more than once every two weeks.

A more normal standard diet for your treefrogs should include gut-loaded crickets, giant mealworms, non-noxious lepidopteran caterpillars (especially silkworms), wax worms, trevoworms, and roaches. Feed your younger frogs daily; adult frogs can be fed every other day. You can leave live foods in with your frogs, but be sure to add a container of their food to the cage. Insects waiting to be eaten get hungry, too.

It should be noted that, if given the opportunity, these two large

A portrait of a male White's treefrog.

treefrogs also will eat smaller frogs (including those of their own species) and small lizards. This should always be kept in mind when you are considering the making of a community terrarium. Choose only same-size cage mates for your White's and white-lipped treefrogs.

Comparatively little has been written about metabolic bone disease (MBD) in captive amphibians. MBD is the reptilian/amphibian equivalent of rickets, and it results when the calcium levels in food are too low and/or when the lack of vitamin D_3 hinders the metabolizing of calcium by your treefrogs. MBD is an insidious problem that will be discussed further in the health section. Both White's and white-lipped treefrogs are known to suffer occasionally from MBD. MBD is a fairly straightforward husbandry/food-related malady that needn't ever be a problem.

Although most of the commercially raised insects utilized for amphibian food will be deficient in calcium, you can supplement their diet once you receive them. Offer them their new diet for 24 hours before you bundle them off to the treefrog cage. Newly fortified with nutritious foods, vitamins, and minerals, your feeder insects become crunchy little ambulatory bonus packages for your frogs. Failing to feed

This White's treefrog sits on a projecting piece of bark.

White's treefrogs often walk slowly along their arboreal highways.

chick-laying mash or the commercial gut-loading food can be made so soupy that it will provide enough water for the insects. Add a small container of water in the crickets' holding cage; we use a small plastic jar lid, and place a short stick in the water (or fill the container with pebbles). Crickets frequently will crawl into any water container and drown; the stick will enable the crickets to climb out.

If you have a large number of treefrogs, you may need to consider the wholesale purchase of food insects. Insect breeders and suppliers advertise in the classifieds in reptile magazines and on the Web. The latter often provides instant on-line ordering opportunities as well. If you need only small numbers of feed insects, your local pet or feed store may be your most economical source. The advantage to buying them locally is that you only buy live insects from your bait or pet store. Any that die in transit from the cricket farm to the pet store, or that die at the pet store, is not your loss. When you order the insects in bulk, some of them may die before you have a chance to use them.

your feeder insects is a little like offering your guests salads made from the yellowed, limp greens you found in the bottom of your refrigerator drawer. It doesn't look good, it doesn't taste good, and it offers nothing in the way of nutrition.

Foods to offer your feed insects include calcium, vitamin D_3 supplements, chick-laying mash (available at your pet or feed store), fresh fruit, grated carrots, squash, broccoli, fresh alfalfa and/or bean sprouts, and honey. A commercially prepared cricket gut-loading diet is now available and it can be used for mealworms and king mealworms, too. Often the

Besides gut loading your food insects, an occasional dusting with a good calcium/D_3 powder may be in order. Just put the insects in a jar with a teaspoon of the vitamin-mineral supplement, cover the jar, and shake it. (This is familiarly called the shake and bake method.) There are several excellent vitamin-mineral supplements now available. Remember that fast-growing baby frogs require a greater amount of calcium than adults.

Selecting Your Treefrogs

Both White's and white-lipped treefrogs are typically heavy-bodied frogs. Some old adults may even be termed corpulent. Despite this, they are strong jumpers and adept climbers. Never purchase a White's or white-lipped treefrog that moves spastically, appears bloated or grossly obese, is too weak to jump or walk steadily, or that has clouded eyes.

Dehydration

Although White's and white-lipped treefrogs are (for amphibians) remarkably resistant to dehydration, occasionally one may escape and evade detection for some time. Resistant to dehydration or not, these frogs do need to be able to replenish missing body moisture. When sufficiently deprived, death will occur. If your frog is still alive when found, remove all dust and dirt by holding it under the tap of your sink. Keep the flow gentle and at room temperature. Place the frog in a closed container (to increase atmospheric humidity) with a shallow covering of dechlorinated water on the bottom. Check on the frog every three hours and return it to its caging when it has recovered enough to sit up and

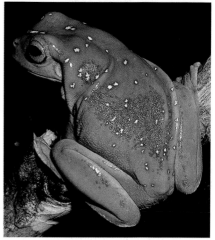

Darkness induces alert behavior in White's treefrogs.

look alert. If the frog is not too dehydrated, it will absorb the needed moisture and recover. The white-lipped treefrog is less able to survive extended periods of dryness than the White's treefrog.

The use of both aerial and topical insecticides and repellents, household cleansers, and hand lotions very quickly will kill your frogs. Do not spray near their cage and never handle your frogs if you are wearing mosquito repellent or any topical insecticide. A great many household and personal cleansers and lotions will

This is a big, somewhat obese, female White's treefrog of Australian origin.

A White's treefrog will often sit quietly on your hand. Wash your hands before and after handling the frog.

prove rapidly fatal to any frog with which they come in contact. Wash your hands carefully, then rinse them thoroughly before touching your treefrogs.

Phenols (pine tar derivatives) are immediately toxic to frogs and never should be used to cleanse terraria or cage furniture.

Gas Bubble Disease

This disease of tadpoles occurs when water is supersaturated with gases. The tadpoles will bloat and a red suffusion will appear on the abdomen and tail. Tadpoles may be unable to submerge. There is no direct cure and the disease can be fatal. Aged water—water allowed to sit in an open container for 24 hours before it is used in an aquarium—will have released its extra gases into the atmosphere, but if fresh water must be used, something as simple as roiling with an airstone or a drip system will help remedy the situation. However, whenever possible, we suggest that aged water be used.

Kidney Disease

Kidney malfunction or disease can cause an irreversible bloating in frogs. The causes are likely manifold, but sitting in unclean water and diets too high in fat seem to be major contributors to this almost invariably fatal problem. It is more often seen in aquatic frogs than in treefrogs, and especially in treefrogs fed an unhealthy diet. (See the comment on feeding your treefrogs pinky mice on page 29.)

Spastic Imbalance

Convulsions, tetanic leg extensions, and lack of coordination also may be due to a multitude of causes, but among these, contamination by unclean water seems to figure prominently. Cleanliness of your frog's quarters is absolutely essential!

Redleg

This is a bacterial disease that can prove rapidly fatal. Since it can be communicable, isolation of infected frogs is mandatory. The bacterial pathogen *Aeromonas* sp. is often but not always implicated. Cleanliness and a suitable temperature regime almost ensures this disease is never encountered; conversely, foul water and land areas, and inordinate chill, will ensure its onset. The causative agent seems to be always present, and only steps in when the frogs' immune systems have been compromised. Tetracycline hydrochloride from your aquarium or pet store is an often-used home remedy (use the dosage suggested for tropical fish), but pathogen

sensitivity tests followed by treatments done by a qualified reptile veterinarian are better.

Cuts, Scrapes, Bruises, and Lesions

These may be of mechanical or bacterial origin. For the former two, a mild antibiotic salve may hasten healing, and the removal of the object causing the injury will prevent recurrence. Nervous frogs, like cricket or chorus frogs, may, when startled, leap repeatedly into the sides of their terrarium (seldom the case with White's or white-lipped treefrogs) and cause recurrent snout bruising. Veterinary assessment is suggested for the lesions. The causative agent must be isolated, identified, and treated.

Intestinal Impaction

This may occur if an overzealous frog ingests gravel or sand while feeding. Small amounts of sand, or an isolated small piece of gravel, is usually passed by the frogs without intervention. Larger impactions may require surgical removal.

Corneal Lipid Buildup

Recently, a form of blindness caused by lipid buildup on the corneas has been seen in frogs that have been fed a diet predominantly of pinky mice. No remedy has been found, but a suitably low-fat (natural) diet would seem to be a preventative.

Fungus Infections

Usually a *Saprolegnia* sp., these may infect the wounds or scrapes of tadpoles. These infections can be treated topically by removing the specimen from the water and daubing hydrogen

A White's treefrog ascends a tree.

This White's treefrog arrived with a badly rubbed nose but needed no medication. The nose healed rapidly when the frog was provided with a secure terrarium.

peroxide (full strength) or malachite green (2%) on the area with a cotton pad. A dilute bath of potassium permanaganate is also useful.

Metabolic Bone Disease (MBD)

This may occur in amphibians that are provided insufficient calcium/D₃ additives in their diets. This is especially true in rapidly growing young specimens. The prevention is simple: feed calcium/D₃ enhanced diets. The cure is less simple. Once sufficiently advanced to be observable, the insidious progression of this deficiency may not be reversible. Consult a veterinarian about injectable calcium treatments. It is possible that these will help.

Endoparasites

Treefrogs collected from the wild may host a number of species of endopara-

sites. These include, among others, subcutaneous nematodes, roundworms, tapeworms, and pinworms. We don't know as yet if all endoparasites are bad for amphibians, or, as with some reptiles, whether endoparasites actually can be beneficial. There are generally no external symptoms other than general listlessness and failure to put on weight, despite a good diet. Because of the virulence of the treatments and the small size of most amphibians, it is best to consult a veterinarian qualified in amphibian medicine for both diagnosis and treatment. Diagnosis is generally made through examination of a fresh (not even refrigerated) stool specimen. In many cases, skin daubs—medications/parasiticides absorbed through the skin of the amphibian—may be preferable to internal purges.

We strongly urge that you find a qualified reptile/amphibian veterinarian before you actually need one. Usually, it is not easy to do so, and it may be too late if your frog is ailing. If your own veterinarian is not a reptile/amphibian specialist, ask for a recommendation. If your veterinarian doesn't know of any local reptile/amphibian veterinarians, check out the web site for the Association of Reptile and Amphibian Veterinarians. Their membership directory link lists reptile/amphibian veterinarians by state.

Breeding

Although herpetoculturists have made great strides in learning how to cycle amphibians reproductively, success in breeding the frogs, toads, treefrogs, salamanders, and caecilians remains far less certain than breeding reptiles. Two principal techniques are used: natural cycling alone, and natural cycling combined with hormonal stimulation. In the former, only natural cues such as winter cooling, seasonally altered rainfall, changing day/night photoperiods, and top-notch health are used. In the latter, following a natural cycling, injectable leutenizing and release hormone (LHRH) is used to enhance the probability of ovulation and spermatogenesis. It should be noted that the LHRH is not a panacea; it will not induce breeding unless all natural cues have been sufficiently duplicated. It is a controlled substance, which means it is not available to the average amphibian hobbyist.

Different breeding cues may be needed by amphibians from different habitats and different latitudes. For example, a treefrog that dwelt all of its life in a tropical latitude, where neither temperature nor day length differs significantly throughout the year, may be cycled reproductively by seasonal fluctuations in rainfall or humidity. Treefrogs from sub-tropical regions may cue in on the rainfall, humidity, photoperiod, and temperature.

Frogs from tropical latitudes breed in ephemeral ponds and waterways. Reproductive cycling of these species seems most largely tied to rainy versus dry season changes, and especially the advent of the first heavy rains of the changing seasons. As the rains fill the seasonally dry puddles, ponds, and creeks, the treefrogs are drawn to these newly freshened breeding sites, which in all probability were their own birthplaces.

Temperate species dependent on ephemeral sites are dependent on the replenishing of the water in their breeding ponds, and upon photoperiod and ambient temperature.

The white-lipped treefrog is a tropical species, as are some of the White's treefrogs. (Some populations of White's from the southern portion of the range decidedly are more of a temperate frog.) White's treefrogs from temperate Australia may require somewhat different cycling methods than those from tropical Indonesia.

White's treefrogs from Australia— if you are certain your strain was originally from Australia—may cycle better if they are hibernated for a period of approximately two months. This can be done in a cool, quiet part of the house—a spare room, or even a cool closet (see page 38 for more specifics on hibernation.) During the cooling period, the frogs may be provided with either a natural photoperiod, or kept in total darkness. During the cooling period, withhold food from the frogs, but make certain that clean water is available. After 60 days, return your frogs to their natural regimen of warmth and care. Feed them heavily. After about a week, begin to use the hydration chamber.

Sexing Your Treefrog

Sexing either White's or white-lipped treefrogs can be a real challenge.

Adult male White's treefrogs often develop a darker throat with "looser" skin than that of the female. The loose skin accommodates the swelling of the vocal sac during cho-rusing. Males are also slightly smaller than the females, and when sitting quietly *may* do so with their forelimbs slightly less flexed than the females. If properly cycled prior to breeding, male White's treefrogs also will develop darkened, roughened nuptial (grasping) pads on the outsides of their thumbs. These pads enable the male to retain his grasp on the female during amplexus (the breeding embrace).

Unless they are actually in re-productive readiness, white-lipped treefrogs are equally difficult to sex. Males are somewhat the smaller sex, and have a darker (often decidedly green) throat. When at the breeding sites, the light stripe on the inside edge of the tibia becomes suffused with a peach hue. Reproductively

ready males of this species also develop darkened, roughened nuptial pads on the outer sides of their thumbs. If males have been cycled properly, a few nights in the hydration chamber usually will bring on the visible sexual color changes.

Cycling Your Treefrogs

How can you ready your White's or white-lipped frogs for breeding? The following procedures usually dupli-cate natural conditions closely enough to stimulate breeding:

1. The adults should be healthy, heavy, and largely endoparasite free.
2. Provide a natural photoperiod. If the animals are kept indoors away from natural light, you can use timers and the times of sunrise and sunset reported in the weather col-umn in your local newspaper to provide a photoperiod that closely resembles the photoperiod where you live. You don't need to change

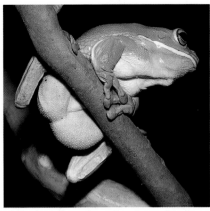

This white-lipped treefrog is tensing for a leap.

the day length on the timer daily; once a week is enough. If there are windows in the room where you keep your frogs, simply turn on the lights at dawn, and turn them off at sunset.

3. Cool the frogs slightly at night, for at least three months during the winter season. Temperatures should range from 55 to 65°F (13 to 18°C) for White's treefrogs of Australian origin, to 68 to 72°F (20 to 22°C) for White's treefrogs of Indonesian origin and white-lipped treefrogs. Those that we kept outdoors in Florida were cooled naturally, with a natural photoperiod.

4. Utilize a hydration chamber, or natural rains in the spring, to trigger reproductive behavior.

More About Cooling

How do you cool down a frog cage? If you live in an area where the temperatures go down into the 50s and 60s (teens on the Celsius scale) at night, just place the frog cage in a cool, darkened part of your house or apartment. A closet shelf may be the right location; a cellar may be just the spot. Even a shelf in a garage or attic may be used. If you're cooling for a lengthy period—meaning more than overnight cooling—be sure that the frog's gut is empty when you put it into its cooling area. Herpetoculturists fear that any food left in a reptile's or amphibian's stomach will putrefy if the animal is cooled or hibernated, and recommend that the animal not be fed for a week or two before it is put into cooling. Clean drinking water should be available at all times, before and during the cooling/hibernation.

What do you do if you live in an area where it doesn't get that cold at

This huge female White's treefrog was imported from New Guinea.

night? First of all, lucky you. Secondly, acquire a second refrigerator: either an apartment-size one or a full-size model is satisfactory. If you aren't picky about how it looks (there are a lot of those harvest gold models around), you can get an inexpensive secondhand one. Then, ask an electrician to change the thermostat on the refrigerator so it will only cool to 55 to 70°F (13 to 21°C). The refrigerator's original thermostat at its highest or warmest setting will still take the temperature inside down to about 40°F (4°C), which is too cold for these treefrogs.

Once you've measured the temperatures on your newly converted refrigerator and made certain they fall within the correct range, set up your hibernaculum. This is a plastic shoebox with holes drilled along the upper edge, just below the edge of the top. Place a folded paper towel on the bottom, and add a thin layer of dried leaves. Put a filled water dish in the corner. Put your gut-cleaned treefrog in the shoebox and replace the lid. Place the shoebox inside the refrigerator. Check the temperature in the refrigerator every day until you're certain that no sudden "cold spells" will set in, and clean/fill up the water bowl as needed, just as you would if you were cooling your frog in your cellar. You'll restore your treefrogs to room temperature at the end of three months.

At the end of the cooling off period, take your frogs out of their cool room/attic/closet shelf/garage/cellar/refrigerator. Place their hibernaculum in the room where you keep their cage, and give them a half day or so to wake up. Put them back in their very clean cage, and begin feeding your treefrogs very heavily. After several days to several weeks of eating well, it's time to breed. The frogs should be heavy, but not obese. Place your treefrogs in the rain chamber (if indoors) or begin misting your outdoor cage or greenhouse in the evenings.

This is one point where those hobbyists who are lucky enough to furnish outdoor caging or greenhouses may be at an advantage. Some herpetoculturists believe that the clutches produced by treefrogs kept in large, outside cages or greenhouses have a better hatch rate and produce somewhat hardier tadpoles than those of frogs stimulated by the more artificial indoor means. Since outdoor facilities are not possible for all herpetoculturists, the indoor cooling sequences and rain chambers are the next best things.

Rain Chambers

The uses and benefits of rain or hydration chambers have long been realized by zoos and other public institutions. They are only now coming into general use by private herpetoculturists and hobbyists. Used in spring or at the start of the rainy season, the chambers mimic the effect of evening rains. They can serve as a trigger in the reproductive cycling of frogs and other amphibians. (A rain chamber also can rehydrate a dehydrated frog, and make the difference between life and death for the frog.)

Making Your Own

A hydration chamber can be constructed of wire mesh over a wood frame, or you may use an aquarium equipped with a circulating water pump and a screen, or perforated Plexiglas top.

If you are fortunate enough to live in a benign climate where the wire cage can be placed outdoors, a mist nozzle can be placed on the end of a hose, affixed over the cage, and fresh water run through this for an hour or more a day.

If indoors, the wire mesh cage can be placed on top, or inside, of a properly drained utility tub and the fresh water system used. It is imperative that the drain system be adequate and kept free of debris if this system is used indoors. A secondary (backup) drain (just in case . . .) might do much to guarantee your peace of mind, and

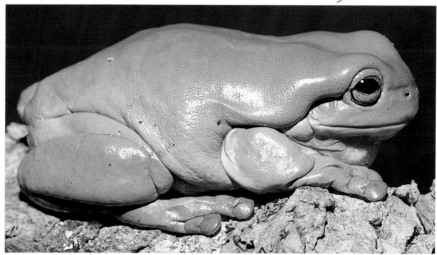
A White's treefrog at rest in its terrarium.

the dryness of your floor. (If your community chlorinates or chloramines the water supply, do not use this method. Opt for the recycled water approach instead.)

In contained systems that use a water pump, water is circulated from the reservoir in the aquarium tank itself through a small-diameter PVC pipe over the top of the tank, into which a series of lateral holes has been drilled. Another method merely brings the water up to the top of the tank and allows it to drip through the screen or perforated Plexiglas top. For obvious reasons, it is imperative that the water in self-contained systems be kept immaculately clean.

When you're ready to deal with breeding and have somewhere to place the eggs (see page 41 for advice on how to deal with more than 1,000 fertilized frog eggs), place your frogs in the misting chamber. Turn on the water or turn on the pump.

One to several hours of misting a night for several (three to seven) evenings should suffice to evoke reproductive behavior in your male and female treefrogs. We suggest that the misting occur in the evenings or early hours of full darkness, since that is the time of day that these treefrogs are most active, and it is also during those hours that they begin gathering at their breeding ponds. If you can't mist at night, at least darken the room where the chamber is located to help duplicate natural conditions. Properly cycled male White's treefrogs will respond to misting by producing an oft-repeated, lengthy series of low-pitched croaks. White-lipped treefrogs produce double croaks. These songs of ardor further stimulate the ovulating females. Amplexus and egg deposition should then follow.

Amplexus

Fertilization of the frog's eggs occurs externally, with the male's sperm being released as the female frog lays her eggs in water. Amplexus is simply the breeding embrace used by the male frog when he finds a cooperative female frog of the same species. The males increase their enthusiasm about breeding by calling or chorusing. After an hour or so, any female within calling range looks pretty good. The male swims or hops over to the female, positions himself on top of her, and holds himself steady by grabbing the female with his front legs. Depending on the species, he may grab behind her front legs, in front of her front legs, or around her waist. As the female lays her eggs, the male fertilizes them. Again, depending on the species, the eggs may float on the surface of the water, or they may clump in masses below the surface of the water.

Care of the Eggs and Tadpoles

The egg masses of both of these treefrogs are laid in the water. The masses normally contain from several hundred to more than 4,000 eggs. These hatch in from two to several days into tiny black tadpoles, which initially cling quietly to the outer jelly of the gelatinous mass, to plants, or to the sides of the deposition receptacle. You cannot possibly provide care, aged water, and food for this number of tadpoles. Select a hundred or so eggs and work to keep them viable. Even with a hundred eggs and a 50 percent hatch rate, you'll have your work cut out for you.

Place the egg mass into an aquarium and provide gentle filtration. Maintain water temperature at 83 to 85°F (28 to 29°C). A tadpole's aquarium should be set up and maintained in precisely the same manner as an aquarium for fish. Water quality,

including the removal of chlorine and chloramine, is very important. Newly hatched tadpoles are weak swimmers, so filtration should not be so strong that they are carried into the mechanism. We have found that sponge canister filters not only provide excellent biological filtration, but the large area of the sponge means the current provided by the pump is not strong enough to trap the tadpoles against the sponge. The sponges are also easily removed and rinsed under a flowing tap to remove detritus.

The eggs should hatch in 1 to 2 days. At first, the tadpoles won't move around much and will lie in place on the sides or the bottom of the tank, absorbing what's left of their yolk sac. After two days, provide food, both animal- and vegetation-based, at least three times a day. Be careful not to provide too much food—even 50 tadpoles can't consume much food, and uneaten food can overwhelm your filter and contaminate the water. Tadpoles will nibble on algae, infusoria, chopped fish, tropical fish flake food, and tadpole food created by the tropical fish food companies. One person swore to me that her tadpoles liked tiny bits of freeze-dried beef liver, the same dog treat she gave her dogs. You'll have plenty of time to try different foods—the tadpoles won't begin to sprout legs and metamorphose until they're about 20 days old.

Infusoria

Infusoria is another word for protozoans. You can "make your own" by placing algae or plants from a quiet stream or pond into a 1-gallon (3.8-L) container of dechlorinated water, and letting the water sit for a few days. This works even better if you can stir in a handful of dried grass, hay, or straw. Protozoans are spread from place to place by the wind, water flow, or animal carriers. Some travel as living protozoans, while others turn into spores. When they end up in a hospitable area—like the quiet water refuge provided in your container of water, with food (deteriorating vegetation or single-celled algae) at hand—the protozoans become active (those in spores emerge from the spores), eat, and look for other like protozoans with whom to mate. These single-celled creatures are too small to catch in any sort of a net—you use an eyedropper to pull up a protozoan-laden water sample from the thickest portion of the weeds or vegetation, and squirt the dropper into a tadpole container.

Metamorphosis

As the tadpoles grow, their swimming ability and agility increase. They begin the massive internal reorganization called metamorphosis. Lungs develop as the gills shrink, and the tadpoles begin rising regularly to the surface to gulp air. The characteristic pouted-lips look of the tadpole is reshaped into a wide, curving mouth; the tail is resorbed as legs form, hidden beneath the skin of the body. First the hind legs pop through; then the front legs.

There will be a pause in feeding as the tail is absorbed. (The nutrients in the tail are used by the froglets, a very practical use of something that's no longer needed.) Once the tail is absorbed, the froglets will be as ravenous as ever. As metamorphosis proceeds, specialized care, such as providing easily accessed haulouts and a lowered water depth, is necessary.

If proper care is afforded, and suitable water quality is maintained, the tadpoles should be fully metamorphosed in 4 to 8 weeks. They'll emerge from the water as tiny replicas of the adults, just under an inch (2.5 cm) in body length. Now you can move them into their adult housing and begin feeding them smaller versions of grown-up food—tiny crickets, fruit flies, springtails, and earthworm pieces. Within a few weeks, these frogs will double in size and you can think about selling them.

Breeding treefrogs, especially the popular species, is a terrific way to help deal with the expenses of acquisition and upkeep. Keep careful notes so you can duplicate positive results and avoid repeating negative results, and consider sharing your techniques with other treefrog fanciers. There's a lot we don't know—yet—about breeding treefrogs, and your contributions would be welcomed.

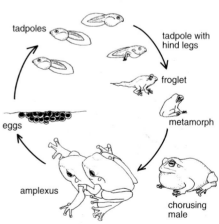

tadpoles

tadpole with hind legs

froglet

metamorph

chorusing male

amplexus

eggs

Life stages in White's treefrog.

Glossary

Aestivation: A period of warm weather inactivity, often triggered by excessive heat or drought.

Ambient temperature: The temperature of the surrounding environment.

Amplexus: The breeding grasp.

Anterior: Toward the front.

Anurans: Tailless amphibians (frogs, toads, and treefrogs).

Anus: The external opening of the cloaca; the vent.

Arboreal: Tree-dwelling.

Caudal: Pertaining to the tail (with tadpoles).

Cloaca: The common chamber into which digestive, urinary, and reproductive systems empty and that itself opens exteriorly through the vent or anus.

Crepuscular: Active at dusk or dawn.

Deposition: As used here, the laying of the eggs.

Deposition site: The spot chosen by the female to lay her eggs.

Dimorphic: A difference in form, build, or coloration involving the same species.

Diurnal: Active in the daytime.

Dorsal: Pertaining to the back; upper surface.

Dorsolateral: Pertaining to the upper sides.

Dorsum: The upper surface.

Genus: A taxonomic classification of a group of species having similar characteristics. The genus falls between the next higher designation of "family" and the next lower designation of "species." "Genera" is the plural of genus. The generic name is always capitalized when written.

Gular: Pertaining to the throat.

Herptiles: A hobbyist vernacular for amphibians and reptiles combined.

Hydrate: To restore body moisture by drinking or absorption.

Hydration chamber: An enclosed high-humidity chamber used to help trigger reproductive behavior in amphibians and to help desiccated frogs rehydrate.

Hylid: A treefrog.

Juvenile: A young or immature specimen.

Labial: Pertaining to the lips.

Lateral: Pertaining to the side.

Lipids: Fats.

Metamorph: Baby anurans, recently transformed from the tadpole stage.

Metamorphosis: The transformation from one stage of life to another.

Middorsal: Pertaining to the middle of the back.

Midventral: Pertaining to the center of the belly or abdomen.

Nocturnal: Active at night.

Nuptial excrescence: The roughened thumb, wrist, and forearm grasping pads of reproductively active male anurans.

Polliwog: Tadpole.

Posterior: Toward the rear.

Species: A group of similar creatures that produce viable young when breeding. The taxonomic designation that falls beneath genus and above subspecies.

Subdigital: Beneath the toes.

Supratympanal: Above the external eardrum (tympanum).

Taxonomy: The science of classification of plants and animals.

Thermoregulate: To regulate (body) temperature by choosing a warmer or cooler environment.

Tympanum: The external eardrum.

Vent: The external opening of the cloaca; the anus.

Venter: The underside of a creature; the belly.

Ventral: Pertaining to the undersurface or belly.

Ventrolateral: Pertaining to the sides of the venter (belly).

Note: Other scientific definitions are contained in the following two volumes:

Peters, James A. *Dictionary of Herpetology*. New York: Hafner Publishing Co., 1964.

Wareham, David C. *The Reptile and Amphibian Keeper's Dictionary*. London: Blandford, 1993.

The white-lipped treefrog is fully at home in shrubs and trees.

Helpful Information

Herpetological Societies

Reptile and amphibian interest groups exist in the form of clubs, monthly magazines, and professional societies, in addition to the herp expos, web pages, and other commercial functions mentioned elsewhere.

Herpetological societies (or clubs) exist in major cities in North America, Europe, and other areas of the world. Most have monthly meetings, some publish newsletters, many host or sponsor field trips and picnics, or indulge in various other interactive functions. Among the members are enthusiasts of varying expertise. Information about these clubs often can be learned by querying pet shop employees, high school science teachers, university biology department professors, or curators or employees at the department of herpetology at local museums and zoos. All such clubs welcome inquiries and new members.

Two of the professional herpetological societies are:

Society for the Study of
   Amphibians and Reptiles (SSAR)
Dept. of Zoology
Miami University
Oxford, OH 45056
http://www.ukans.edu/~ssar

Herpetologist's League
c/o Texas Nat. Heritage Program
Texas Parks and Wildlife Dept.
4200 Smith School Rd.
Austin, TX 78744

The SSAR publishes two quarterly journals: *Herpetological Review* contains husbandry, range extensions, news about ongoing field studies, and so on, while the *Journal of Herpetology* contains articles more oriented toward academic herpetology.

Hobbyist magazines that publish articles on all aspects of herpetology and herpetoculture (including treefrogs) are:

Reptiles
P. O. Box 6050
Mission Viejo, CA 92690
http://animalnetwork.com/reptiles/default.asp

Reptile and Amphibian Hobbyist
Third and Union Aves.
Neptune City, NJ 07753
http://www.tfh.com

Hobbyist magazines also carry classified ads and news about herp expos.

Index